Defuse:
7 Steps to Saving Your 401(k) from the IRS

Dan Cuprill, CFP®

*Foreword by Jerry Royer, RFC® and
Nicholas Royer, MRFC*

Beyond the Fine Print

Any time you pick up a book about personal finance, and you understand some, most, or all of it, this may have absolutely nothing to do with your financial situation. In several cases, the author made assumptions, and if those assumptions don't apply to you, neither does the advice.

Before you even consider implementing any of the recommendations in this book, please consult a professional advisor.

Free Bonus

To help you get a better understanding of this extremely important topic, the authors have created a membership website that has a comprehensive video training program and all the resources and links from this book.

The great news is access to the site is 100% FREE. You can get it at DefuseTheTaxBomb.com.

Here is what you'll receive:

1. A comprehensive Video Series that breaks down the strategies inside Defuse (NOTE: You'll also get access to Advanced Content not found in the book).

2. A series of PDF's to help you implement the strategies in the book.

3. Complete resources from the book.

4. Private access to a complimentary Strategy Session by Phone with Jerry or Nick Royer to dive deeper into how to make these strategies work for you. Call 1-800-245-0546 or schedule your

time or use their online calendar at
www.Group10Financial.com

To get started, go to
www.DefuseTheTaxBomb.com

Foreward by Jerry Royer, RFC® and Nicholas Royer, MRFC

You're FIRED!!!

Isn't this basically what happens the moment you retire? Retirement is like 20-30 years of unemployment. Are you ready? Do you know how to be ready? Do you know what landmines await you on your financial battlefield?

For some people retirement is awesome, for others...retirement sucks. What's the difference between these two? The difference is the right kind of knowledge, the right kind of preparation, and the right kind of planning.

Unfortunately, how to retire awesome is not a topic taught in high schools. It's not even a topic taught in colleges. Companies don't teach their employees about money. Then you retire and you're thrown out of the safe confines of the working world only to rely on what you've saved to get you through the next few decades of your life.

Shouldn't retirement be filled with certainty, simplicity, and financial confidence? Why isn't it for many Americans?

During a national conference a few months back, a friend of ours introduced us to someone who felt the exact same way as we did. He too was passionate about helping people avoid making critical mistakes in retirement and helping them put an end to paying unnecessary taxes. We saw the challenges that retirees have from the same light. We saw a world where most retirees have invested in a way where most of their life savings is just a ticking tax time bomb waiting to explode, especially if taxes go up in the future (which they likely will). That person was Dan Cuprill.

Taxes aren't the only landmines that can blow up your retirement. Stock market crashes, healthcare expenses, running out of money before you run out of life, inflation, estate issues, etc. etc. are all possible landmines retirees may face. These risks are endless, and unfortunately, way too many retirees are making the same mistakes over and over again.

Einstein once said, "We cannot solve our problems with the same level of thinking that created them."

What you have in front of you is the retirement blueprint you need to help you create a financial house that can weather any storm, no matter what Washington or Wall Street throws at you.

This book is going to test the way you look at retirement, money, and taxes. It's going to help rescue you from the landmines that we see blow finances to shreds during the retirement years.

However, where others have failed, you can now succeed because you'll be armed with the knowledge they never had.

Once you read this book, you'll know how to rescue your retirement from the IRS and disinherit them from your money legally, morally, and ethically. Your learning won't stop just at taxes. You'll also find out many other pro-tips to help make sure your retirement is filled with confidence, fun, and certainty.

So dive right in and start making a transformational difference in your financial life so you can "Fire" Uncle Sam from his control over your money.

Jerry Royer, RFC® and Nicholas Royer, MRFC
Radio Show Co-Hosts
Founders of Group 10 Financial, LLC

FREE TOOLKIT REVEALS How to Avoid Paying Unnecessary Taxes On Your 401(k), IRA, 403(b) or TSP in Retirement

For a limited time, you can get your own FREE copy of this Tax-Free Retirement Toolkit shipped direct to your doorstep at no cost.

✓ How to create a Tax-Free Retirement Plan.

✓ The Top 10 Things to consider for your retirement.

✓ The 5 Mistakes you must avoid with your money.

✓ How to build a plan that works in both good and sour markets.

Claim Your Toolkit Now

TEXT **RETIRE** **TO** **31996**

Or call 1.800.245.0546

About Jerry Royer, RFC® and Nicholas Royer, MRFC

Jerry and Nick Royer are keynote speakers, authors, radio show hosts, and consumer advocates who have been featured on both NBC and ABC News Networks.

Known as America's Father & Son Financial Coaches, they have been fiercely dedicated to helping people make smart financial decisions to help them get to and through retirement.

Their nationally syndicated Gold Record winning **On The Money with Jerry & Nick Royer Radio Show** was the answer to the growing epidemic of so many Americans suffering from the same financial landmines in retirement over and over again.

Jerry, Nick, and their team have already helped hundreds of families over the last 53 years rescue their retirement so they can defuse or altogether avoid those financial landmines...no matter what Washington or Wall Street throws at them.

This is Not a Drill!

A bomb is about to explode, and you must take precautions. Again, this is NOT a drill.

Sadly, our world is much more complicated today. Do you remember a time when going to work didn't require a security badge? You could arrive at the airport 30 minutes before your flight and walk through security fully clothed, bags intact. You felt safe going to the movies. Kids played outside all day, their parents having no idea where they were and they didn't worry about it.

Yes, sadly, those days are over.

We can attribute much of that change to a growing population. In your lifetime, the global population has probably doubled. And it may double again before you die. Nashville was once a sleepy little town. Now it's a booming one, known to many as NashVegas. Ditto for Phoenix, Charlotte, San Antonio, and most of Florida.

A bigger world is a complex world, one with lots of challenges. What worked in the past with a small population doesn't always work with one so massive.

Horrible crimes are not a modern phenomena, but they do occur more frequently (and receive a lot more publicity with 24-hour cable news).

What worked back then doesn't work today. Not airport security, not kids playing unsupervised, and not many facets of our government.

The one area most affected by our population explosion has been entitlements: Social Security and Medicare in particular. Once a "contract with our seniors," these programs are now being described as "fiscal cancers" by the very people responsible for making them work. We'll discuss that in detail. Today, we have far more people receiving benefits than ever before, and the percentage of workers supporting them has never been smaller. And it's getting smaller every day.

So far, the government's solution to fixing the Social Security problem has been a number of band-aid measures:

- Push back the age for full benefits
- Lower inflation increases
- Tax the benefits

- Raise the contribution amounts of working Americans

These are minor fixes, akin to "kicking the can down the road." The real problem is we built the system using a structure that is illegal in the non-government world. It's called a "Ponzi Scheme." More on that to come.

In 1984, House Speaker Tip O'Neil introduced the idea of taxing Social Security benefits as a way to lower them without sparking the ire of the American Association of Retired People (AARP), arguably Washington's strongest lobby group. The government didn't lower benefits, but by taxing them for one-third of Americans, they essentially did the same thing. Ironically, when you contribute money to Social Security, you cannot deduct it from your taxes. So, for many Americans, paying tax on benefits is akin to paying tax twice on the same money. In criminal law, this is called "double jeopardy," prevented by the constitution. In tax law, it's standard operating procedure.

If you are married and have a retirement of more than $44,000, it's highly likely you pay tax on as much as 85% of your Social Security check.

If you have money in a 401(k), 403(b), or Traditional IRA, you have yet to pay tax on it. Withdrawing some of it during retirement will not only trigger tax on that money, but it will also affect the taxation of your Social Security benefits. In other words, you get less. Consider it Washington's way of cutting Social Security without having the courage to say so.

The amount of tax you will pay on your retirement income will depend on the rates set at that time. In late 2017, President Trump signed a bill lowering taxes in hopes it would stimulate economic growth. It probably will, and in doing so, treasury revenues will rise. But will they rise enough to pay the ever-growing needs of the government? Presently our nation owes over $20 trillion.

As financial advisors, we worry about a lot of things. It's an occupational hazard. The stock market decline, inflation rates, interest rates, clients outliving their money. But nothing keeps us awake more than the fact few people today have traditional pension plans. Instead, people (like you) have things like 401(k)'s and IRA's. How well these plans will grow is unknown, not to mention how they will be taxed.

Will tax rates be lower in your retirement than they are at this moment? Could this most recent tax cut be the bottom? What if rates have to rise? What impact will it have on you and all that money that has yet to be taxed? We'll consider this question.

Fortunately, strategies do exist to counter this threat. Good strategies. Proven strategies. Strategies that can rescue your retirement, provide you a tax-free retirement, and help you to defuse the ticking tax time bomb that awaits so many of our future retirees.

Let's meet two of them...Harry and Sally Burns.

When Harry Met Sally

If you saw the movie When Harry Met Sally, then there's no need to bring up the infamous diner scene or the awkwardness Harry felt when the two crossed the line from friends to lovers (and if you haven't seen the movie, do so. It's one of Rob Reiner's few good ones).

Our story today picks up where the movie left off. Harry and Sally are no longer young urban hipsters. They're now like the older couples who told stories at the start of the movie about how they met.

They are now recently retired. Sally has $750,000 in an IRA. Harry another $500,000 in his former company's 401(k). The kids have left the nest, no more mortgage debt, and our favorite couple is excited about leaving New York and moving to the tax haven of Nashville, TN.

In addition to having no state income tax, Tennessee also has very low property taxes. Our couple feels very good about this decision. Their financial advisor also thinks it's a wonderful idea.

17

Their paid-off Upper East Side condo will sell for more than the cost of a new house in Nashville.

The Burns' believe they can live comfortably on $6,000 a month, half of which will come from Social Security. The rest will come from their $1.25 million in savings.

Their advisor is comfortable with the payout amount given the size of their savings. Invested wisely, they should have no worries about running out of money in their lifetime. Life is good!

Every month, he wires $3,000 to the Burns's account. Like clockwork. But when their investment statement arrives, Harry notices that $4,000 is withdrawn each month, not $3,000. He anxiously calls for an explanation.

Are Harry and Sally victims of another Bernie Madoff?

"Relax, Harry," says the advisor. "Remember, you have yet to pay tax on that money, so every time you make a withdrawal, we have to send the IRS its cut."

"But 25%?" asks Harry. "Isn't that a lot on just $3,000 a month? Aren't we living in a tax-free state?"

"Oh sure, you don't have to pay any state income taxes, but the federal government still gets it cut. And you have to pay tax on your Social Security check. Add that to the interest you're getting on some of your savings accounts and your total tax bill will be about $12,000 a year. But don't worry, we already factored that in."

And so it goes.

Life continues to be good, until one day when his advisor calls again.

"Harry, as you may know, the new administration instituted a tax increase. So, we're going to need to start taking out $4,500 a month to send you $3,000. Unless of course, you and Sally think you can live on less than $3,000."

Harry responds, "No. In fact, we've never increased it for inflation, so I'd like to start getting $3,200 a month."

"Okay, well, in that case, we need to start withdrawing $4,550 to give you $3,200 a month. I'll send you the paperwork."

About a year later, Harry notices his account is down about 10%. Another call to his advisor.

"Yeah, we've seen some volatility lately. It's normal," the advisor says. "Markets always come back eventually."

"But are we going to have enough?" asks Harry. I mean, we're now taking more money than we used to and our balance is less. Isn't that going to be a problem?'

There's now silence on the end of the line. Finally, the advisor speaks, "Harry, let me run some numbers and get back you."

The advisor calls back later that day.

"Here's the thing Harry. We anticipated markets would drop at some point. They always do. But they always come back. We also expected you to need to take an increase now and then to keep up with inflation. We factored that in as well. But what I didn't anticipate was this huge tax increase. No one could. It's unprecedented. Sure, I think markets will come back, but in the meantime, we have to sell more shares now than we did last year to give you $3,200. So, even though markets will probably come back, these extra shares we're selling are gone."

"So what does this mean?"

Well, it means you and Sally will have to cut back. I'm thinking to about $2,800 a month, at least until things settle down. Otherwise, you could run out of money."

Now, I'm not going to get all Steven King on you and tell you that Harry is now working as a Wal-Mart greeter while Sally is waitressing at Waffle House until something snaps and Penny Wise the Clown feeds them to a giant spider.

No, the story doesn't need to go that far to emphasize the point that added to inflation and market volatility, taxes can have a crippling effect on your retirement. That is, of course, unless you do something about it.

When Charlie met Otto

Let's go back in time. It's now 1920. In a small office on 27 School Street in Boston, Carlo Pietro Guglielmo Tebaldo Ponzi, known to his friends as Charlie, begins his own investment business. Seventeen years prior, he arrived in America from Italy with only $2.50 in his pocket. Now he's about to take advantage of large currency fluctuations following The Great War. By buying and selling something called an International Reply Coupon (IRC), Ponzi figures out a way to make a true arbitrage profit. It was almost like Newman and Kramer's idea to return New York's 5 cent deposit cans to Michigan for a 10 cent refund (My apologies if you never watched Seinfeld).

The only problem was Ponzi lacked cash. So, he starts seeking investment from the public, promising to double their money in 90 days or less.

Early on, Charlie delivered big time, paying as much as $750 dividend on an investment of $1,250. By July of 1920, total investment in

Charlie's "scheme" reaches $1 million a day. That's big money now. Imagine what it was in 1920.

Charlie Ponzi, the once fired waiter and Italian immigrant, is now a multi-millionaire. Investors love him, some going as far as mortgaging their homes to invest more. Rather than take their interest payments, many just rolled them into another investment of IRC.

Here's the problem: Charlie wasn't making huge returns on IRC's. In fact, he's not buying IRC's at all. He never figured how to convert IRC's to cash. But that didn't daunt him. As long as the new money kept flowing in, Charlie could pay old investors with the money from new ones.

Of course, Charlie started to enhance his lifestyle. He bought a mansion in suburban Lexington as well as the finest car of that time, a Locomobile (translation: crazy car). He planned to donate $100,000 to charity and even bought a macaroni and wine company. He hoped these companies would allow him to pay off his investors since the IRC idea didn't work.

Eventually, the new money stopped coming in. Investors started asking for their money and the mother of all pyramid schemes, the Ponzi scheme, failed. By the end of 1920, authorities sent Charlie to prison for fraud.

Ponzi may have had the best of intentions when he started his enterprise, but he quickly learned that even in America, success doesn't come easy. If it did, everyone would have it.

So how did a college dropout from Italy conspire such a scheme in the New World?

He's not the first one to try. In fact, the best example of this type of pyramid scheme can be traced back to Germany just 40 years earlier.

Otto Von Bismark is considered Germany's George Washington. Before unification, Germany was an assortment of city-states. Under the order of Emperor Wilhelm I, Bismark created a social insurance program designed to offer financial support to the elderly. Ironically, he was a stout anti-socialist but offered the new program as a way to appease the growing support for communism coming out of Russia. His Social Insurance program offered a monthly stipend to people once they reached age 70.

Ponzi wasn't the only person to learn from Bismark. In 1937, Franklin D. Roosevelt created a similar scheme called Social Security. The idea was simple. Workers would contribute 1% of the first $3,000 they make every year to the program. Their employer would match it. For everyone receiving a check, there would be 42 people putting money in. What could go wrong? Back then the average life expectancy was under 60. You had to wait until 65 to receive benefits. And if you did live that long, you rarely lived past 70. If FDR's Social Security system was a Ponzi scheme, it was a very good one.

Enter another German statesman who would create a series of ripple effects, the least of which on Social Security. Nonetheless, Adolf Hitler left his mark here as well.

Sixteen million Americans, mostly young men between 18 and 30, served in World War II. When they returned, they married and started having children at record rates. The Baby Boomer Generation had begun. America's largest generation, those born between 1946-1964, would transform the US like none prior. In some ways good, in other ways...well, we have to blame disco on someone.

So large is the Baby Boomer generation that today there are only three people putting money into

Social Security for every Boomer getting a check. And contrary to what many think, Social Security deposits are NOT placed in an account for your future consumption. Quite the contrary. As soon as you put money into the system, almost all of it is re-routed to a retiree. Remember....in 1937, there were 42 contributors for every recipient. Now there are 3. And in ten years there will be only 2. That's more than the loss of just one person. It's a decline of one third the total contributors. It took a while, but Social Security is on track to face the same fate as Charlie Ponzi's investors.

Of course, no one is going to jail.

After FDR, another US president took the stakes even higher and created Medicare. When he wasn't escalating the Vietnam War, Lyndon B. Johnson instituted a single-payer healthcare system for America's elderly using the same model of Bismark and Ponzi. In his book, Comeback America, former US Comptroller David M. Walker predicts Medicare will cost five times more than Social Security. Without a population base to support it, Walker predicts taxes will have to double. Did you get that? Double.

Sound unlikely? Keep reading.

The Code

As you may recall, the founders of the United States were a bunch of tax-weary renegades, angry at not having parliamentary representation. King George III bankrupted Great Britain by fighting the French for the umpteenth time and needed cash to prepare for the next battle. So, he started taxing his colonies heavily. After all, isn't the purpose of a colony to serve the mainland?

Fortunately, these rebels had some pretty smart people amongst them. Geniuses actually. Men with such foresight they decided to create an elected republic rather than a monarchy after defeating the British. The rest of the world soon followed, and today Great Britain's royal family can't even marry without the blessings of Parliament. Don't feel sorry for them. Other monarchs faced far worse fates.

When the founders wrote the US Constitution, they did so in a way that strongly limited the role of the federal government (much to the displeasure of future politicians). In fact, they didn't even allow for an income tax. That required the 16th amendment. [The Supreme Court rules passed efforts to tax income as unconstitutional because the founders did not afford that power.] Think of it...judges ruled on what the constitution said, not what they wanted it to say.

Most taxes discourage the activity that generates the tax. For example, taxes on cigarettes are meant to discourage people from smoking. Gas taxes discourage excessive use of fuel. The income tax is much different. It taxes your ability to survive. Little wonder it wasn't part of Madison's Constitution.

Nonetheless, the income tax isn't going anywhere. If you choose to act like Wesley Snipes and pretend it doesn't apply to you, jail awaits.

Still kinder than King George III, but our government sets the terms for freedom.

A Walk Down Memory Lane
Upon ratification of the 16th Amendment, Congress issued the first Revenue Act of 1913, levying a tax of 1% on incomes above $3,000 and a 6% tax on incomes over $500,000. Ah, the good old days. But soon politicians decided 6% wasn't

enough. In five years, the tax rate reached 77% to fund World War I. In the 1930's, the top rate was 63%. In 1945, it hit 94% on incomes over $200,000. In the 1970's, the top rate was 70%. Add to that state income taxes, and many American paid more than half their earnings to the government.

In his now famous speech to the Economic Club of New York, President John F. Kennedy proposed an income tax reduction as a way to stimulate the economy, much as future presidents Reagan and Trump would likewise initiate.

Done properly, lower taxes can result in more treasury revenue because of expanded economic activity. The IRS may get a smaller piece of the pie, but the pie is larger.

Of course, nothing can stop Congress from spending more than the country makes. So even with rising revenues, deficits can and do exist.

In the short run, higher taxes can result in more government revenue, but in the long run, a country cannot tax itself into prosperity. Google the USSR, Greece, Venezuela, and Cuba for proof. Eventually, you run out of other people's money as Lady Thatcher famously observed.

But enough with common sense. Historically, higher tax rates are the norm, but we are presently living in a period of very low ones. Only a few hundred votes in Pennsylvania prevented us from witnessing a tax increase instead of a cut in 2017.

Will taxes rise in the future? No one knows for certain, but the demographical shifts described in the last chapter suggest it's inevitable.

Every day 10,000 Baby Boomer turn 65. In ten years, almost 20% of our population will receive a Social Security check. Add to that the interest we must pay to service our debt on top of our growing needs for infrastructure repair and healthcare, and it doesn't look promising.

Which now brings us back to Harry and Sally.

Like most baby boomers, they haven't yet paid tax on most of their nest egg. While as retirees they may be in a lower bracket than when they worked, that rate can change over time. If it's higher than their advisor projected, they will have less money. Add to that inflation and typical stock market fluctuations, and baby boomers like the Burns are extremely vulnerable.

Does it make sense to have 100% of one's retirement savings vulnerable to the whims of Congress and future presidents? Do you think a President Sanders would lower taxes? How about a President Warren or a President Cuomo? How likely is it that any Congress will suggest a reduction in spending? Heck, just lowering the increase in spending is considered a tax cut in Washington. Before you conclude I'm being political, let's look at the words of a Clinton appointee who served under George Bush.

A Prophet Named Dave

To borrow from the Holy Bible, no one is a prophet in his hometown.

Unless you're the former head of the General Accounting Office, the country's CPA. Then people tend to take notice.

Appointed by President Clinton in 2003, David M. Walker also served under President Bush. If he has a partisan bone in his body, it's not toward political ideology, but math.

Since 2007, Walker has been touring the country espousing the need for fiscal responsibility. His strategy is one that neither liberals or conservatives will like: Raise Taxes AND Cut Spending.

As stated previously, what drives the problem behind our growing national debt and future obligations (which, as of 2018, are about $80 trillion), is our demographics. The Baby Boomer generation retires 10,000 people a day. They are leaving the workforce (where they paid both payroll and income taxes) and are now receiving

Social Security and Medicare. Contrary to what the AARP wants people to think, no one has fully paid for their entitlements. Current taxation subsidizes most of it. You may have helped pay for someone else's Medicare, but not yours.

Walker's book, Comeback America, lays out the argument quite succinctly. Tax rates need to double. At one time, Congress controlled almost every dollar the government spends. Today, it's about a third. Debt interest, Social Security, Medicare, and Medicaid are locked in expenses. They aren't up for negotiation. Unless things change, Walker predicts by 2040, treasury revenues will be only enough to cover debt interest (which is the fastest growing expense. Medicare is second.) and a small percentage of retirement benefits.

He even goes as far as calling Medicare, the health plan for the elderly, a fiscal cancer. Medicare costs are five times greater than Social Security. People are living longer and receiving unlimited care.

How likely is it someone will get elected with the following platform:

1. Double income taxes.
2. Increase the payroll tax to 100% of earnings.
3. Reduce Social Security for anyone with a taxable income over $50,000.
4. Eliminate Social Security cost of living adjustments.
5. Deny Medicare claims for hip replacements, knee replacements, and most drugs for anyone over age 80.

If the Tea Party doesn't kill the candidate, AARP most certainly will.

More doom and gloom to consider. Foreign countries, mostly China, own a fifth of our debt. What if they stop lending us money? What if the interest rate on our current debt rises?

The US government doesn't get to file Chapter 11. And I doubt quite seriously they ever will need to.

Economic growth can offset some of the deficit, but will it be enough? Few economists think so.

Walker has very few critics. Politicians on both sides agree they need to act. Few, if any, dare to lead the way.

If given a choice: cutting taxes OR cutting benefits, I think it's a safe bet which is more politically feasible, so long as the Baby Boomers live.

Taxes are highly likely to rise in the future. As Walker says, there's a four letter word that makes it inevitable: Math

When they do, will you be ready?

Harry and Sally Get Help

Since we're using movie characters as the basis for our story, let's do a little rewrite. Instead, let's pretend Harry and Sally had a different discussion with their advisor, this one set about ten years before they retired. Here's how that meeting could have gone (or should have gone).

Advisor: It's great seeing you both. Sally, you don't age. Heck, you look just like John Mellencamp's girlfriend.

Sally: Oh, stop.

Advisor: Well, I'm really glad you two came in. Looking at my records, it appears you are now ten years away from retirement. Still want to leave work at 65?

Harry: Yes, I think so. We'd like to get out of the city and go somewhere quiet. We recently visited some friends in Nashville and liked it there.

Advisor: Good choice. Great entertainment, close to some awesome trout streams, and no state income tax. Property taxes are low, too.

Sally: And the housing market looks good as well. But, do you think we'll have enough?

Advisor: In theory, yes I do. There will always be obstacles, but I think you'll have enough. I do recommend we start doing some restructuring form a tax perspective.

Harry: Such as?

Advisor: Well, right now almost all of your money is in your 401(k) and IRA accounts.

Sally: Right. We're trying to pay as little tax as possible. By maxing our 401(k) contributions, we're lowering our income taxes.

Advisor: You're lowering your current income taxes. That's true. But you will have to pay those taxes in the future. I worry tax rates could be higher when you retire than the present given how our government likes to spend money. No one has a crystal ball, but would it make sense to move some of your money from "taxed later" accounts like your 401(k) to a "taxed never account?"

Harry: You mean like a Roth IRA.

Advisor: Actually, a Roth IRA is just one such vehicle, but it might make sense. We should at least consider it. Do you agree?

Sally: Yes!

Advisor: Okay, but you need to understand something first. There is no such thing as a free lunch. You will pay the tax. The question is when. We presently have the lowest federal tax rates in your lifetime. If I create a strategy to give you a lower or even a tax-free retirement, it may require you pay more taxes now to achieve it. Are you okay with that?

Harry: How much more?

Advisor: Hard to say, but your REAL net worth will remain unchanged.

Sally: What does that mean?

Advisor: Your accounts today are worth about $625,000. But in truth, you don't have that much. The IRS has yet to take its cut. When you pull the money out, you must pay tax. So, your real net worth is what you have left after the IRS gets its share. In reality, you have about $450,000.

My point is that even though you may pay some tax now to move some of your money to tax-free, the amount you have after tax will remain unchanged. Furthermore, going forward, all future growth in the tax-free strategy will remain tax-free.

Harry: But doesn't it make sense to keep delaying the tax?

Advisor: If we knew for certain taxes in the future won't skyrocket, then it probably would. We don't know. I see a country with lots of debt and aging Baby Boomers. I can't help but ask, shouldn't we take advantage of these low rates and move some money now? Wouldn't a little balance make sense?

Harry: When do we start?

The Seven Steps to a
Tax-Free Retirement

Few strategies will work for everyone. There are upsides and downsides to every one of them. As I stated earlier, what follows is meant to be educational. Do not accept it as advice. Consult your advisor before proceeding.

Harry and Sally live in New York City, one of the most tax abusive places in the country. Since every state is different, I've chosen to NOT include state and local income taxes as a consideration for the strategies that follow. But you, however, MUST consider them. Hopefully, your city and state will make at least one of these strategies a logical one.

Ten years before retirement, Harry and Sally's financial picture looks like this:

Cash: $150,000

Sally's 401(k): $375,000

Harry's IRA: $250,000

Total: $775,000

At 65, their planned retirement age, they'll both receive about $1,500/month in Social Security benefits.

Also, they both have $1 million of term insurance, for which they pay a combined premium of $3,200.

Assuming they average 7% return on their investments in the next ten years, their retirement accounts will double in value. We'll assume they still have $150,000 in cash at age 65. So, as we mentioned earlier, their investments at age 65 will be:

Cash: $150,000

Sally's 401(k): $750,000

Harry's IRA: $500,000

Total: $1,400,000

A nice balance. They should feel very good about retirement.

But from a tax perspective, there's reason to worry.

First, they have not yet paid tax on 90% of their liquid assets. How much will the IRS eventually get? We have no idea, remember? But we worry it could be more than expected.

All we know is their current savings are vulnerable. If we divided them up by tax status, here's how they look:

When Will It Be Taxed?

Now?	Later?	Never?
$150,000	$1,250,000	$0

Although bank accounts don't pay much interest, whatever Harry and Sally receive will be taxed. And when they start pulling money out of their IRA and 401(k)s, that too will be taxed. On top of that, they must also pay tax on their Social Security benefits.

Will you pay tax on your Social Security benefits? To answer this question, we begin by first calculating the Modified Adjusted Gross Income (MAGI). The MAGI is ½ of Social Security benefits plus any other sources of income (wages, 401(k)/IRA withdrawals, interest, dividends). For married couples, if the MAGI exceeds $32,000,

Uncle Sam gets a piece of the Social Security check. For a single person, tax on benefits begins when the MAGI reaches $25,000. For more details, go to Appendix I.

Example: Harry and Sally will receive combined Social Security benefits of $36,000. Also, they have 36,000 in 401(k) withdrawals. Their MAGI is: $54,000 ($18,000 (1/2 of SS benefits) + $36,000 IRA withdrawals). So, part of their Social Security benefit will be taxed.

Once the MAGI exceeds $44,000, Harry and Sally can pay tax on as much as 85% of the Social Security benefit.

If they didn't have to pay tax on Social Security, their federal tax bill would be only $940. Instead it's $2,487. Even worse, as their advisor pointed out, they've already paid tax once on this money. Now they pay it again. Thank you, Tip O'Neil!

To protect themselves against future tax increases and shield their Social Security benefits from taxation, Harry and Sally can employ some strategies that work best when started before retirement. Like all strategies, none is perfect. Each has a cost or downside. But they may be better than doing nothing. With each of these approaches, the idea is to pay the tax at current rates and not later in life when rates could be higher.

1. Fund a Roth 401(k): Some employer 401(k) plans give you the choice of contributing to either a traditional or Roth 401(k). If traditional, then contributions to the plan are not taxed until withdrawn. Traditional (pre-tax) accounts comprise the overwhelming majority of 401(k) assets. Tax is paid later, not now.

2. With a Roth 401(k), you contribute after-tax money, but future growth and withdrawals are tax-free taken after age 59.%. Tax is paid now, not later. In other words, income taken from a Roth 401(k) is tax-free. Also, your MAGI does factor in Roth withdrawals. Hence, they don't affect the taxation of your Social Security benefits. *See Appendix I.*

3. Fund a Roth IRA: Depending on your age and income, you can contribute up to $6,500 into a Roth IRA every year.

Contributions are not tax-deductible, but like the Roth 401(k), withdrawals are fully tax-free if completed after age 59.5. *For more details on the Roth, see Appendix II.*

4. Convert to a Roth IRA: This one is cute. Uncle Sam doesn't like waiting for his taxes, so if you'd like, you can convert money sitting in your traditional or rollover IRA to a Roth at any time. In doing so, you agree to pay taxes now on whatever you convert. You don't have to covert it all. All after-conversion money will be free of taxation. Conversion can be a very powerful strategy, but you MUST have a full understanding of the taxes you will have to pay to convert. Hire a professional! *See Appendix III for more details.*

5. Use IRC 72(t): Another tricky one. In most cases, money taken from an IRA before age 59.5 will result in a 10% tax penalty on top of the tax you'll owe on what you take out. There is a way around this. Depending on your age, you can withdraw a certain amount every year without paying the

penalty. It's the Equal and Substantial amount. Once you start withdrawing, you must take that same amount out every year for five years or until you reach age 59.5, whichever comes last. Once removed, money can then be placed into a tax-free vehicle or used for conversion. Again, hire a professional before proceeding. *More details on this concept are in Appendix IV.*

6. Cash Value Life Insurance: Until the Roth IRA, only life insurance gave you the opportunity to grow your money tax-deferred AND access it tax-free via policy loans and withdrawals. Unfortunately, the growth of many policies is limited by low-interest rates and internal fees. While I rarely recommend a couple like Harry and Sally buy a cash value product in their 50's, the tax benefits may be a reason to keep their existing policy in place. Newer cash value policies often have another feature worth considering (which is why I sometimes do recommend them): Long Term Care coverage. Rather than wait for death, some policies will pay a living benefit

to cover the cost of custodial health care coverage. *More details on this in Appendix V.*

7. Now that we know what we can do within the restraints of the US tax code, it's time to develop a strategy.

Step One: Know your marginal tax bracket.
A little Tax 101. Don't worry...it's not that painful. Remember, it's your money, so it's worth it.

Here's how it works. As a married couple, Harry and Sally are allowed to have their first $24,000 tax-free. And since they're over age 65, they can shelter another $2,500. So, Uncle Sam doesn't start collecting until earnings exceed $26,500. Even Oprah gets a holiday.

The tax they will pay depends on how much over $26,500 they earn in a given year. So, if total earnings are $46,000, subtract $26,500. That leaves $19,500 of taxable income. Tax owed is 10% or $1,950.

Rate	Individuals	Married Filing Jointly
10%	Up to $9,525	Up to $19,050
12%	$9,526 to $38,700	$19,051 - $77,400
22%	38,701 to $82,500	$77,401 - $165,000
24%	$82,501 to $157,500	$165,001 - $315,000
32%	$157,501 to $200,000	$315,001 - $400,000
35%	$200,001 to $500,000	$400,001 - $600,000
37%	over $500,000	over $600,000

It's important to understand how much additional income you can have without jumping to a higher bracket.

Important Point: It is not your total income that matters, but your TAXABLE INCOME. Again, taxable income is what you earn minus your allowable deductions.

Step Two: Generate only enough additional income to stay in your marginal bracket.
A married couple in the 12% marginal bracket can have a taxable income of $77,400 and remain in that bracket. Let's assume they're at $65,000.

This means they could earn another $12,400 and still pay only 12% tax on that additional income.

Ideally, any tax planning strategy such as a Roth Conversion or reducing 401(k) contributions should attempt to keep the taxpayer in their present bracket. If that's not possible, then it's important to know in advance the additional tax.

Step Three: Set aside cash reserves equal to six months of living expenses.
Cash reserves are the basic foundation of a financial strategy. A major reason why so many Americans swim in debt is a failure to build up cash reserves to protect themselves against unexpected expenses or loss of income.

For most people, three to six months of living expenses is an adequate amount of cash to keep in a bank account. Any more than that and it's likely the paltry return banks pay will be less than the compounded effects of taxes and inflation on that interest.

For Harry and Sally, six months of living expenses are $60,000. This leaves them with $90,000 to start implementing a tax-free retirement strategy.

Step Four: Reduce traditional 401(k) contributions.
The 401(k) plan is a very effective way to save for retirement. As I stated earlier, money contributed is deducted from your current income, hence lowering your current tax bill. Even better, many employers match a part of your contribution. FREE MONEY.

Starting a traditional 401(k) is rarely a bad thing. It's when it gets too large that one should consider alternative strategies to lower the vulnerability to future tax rates.

One option is to invest 401(k) contributions into a Roth 401(k). They look and smell just like a regular 401(k), except you can't deduct your contributions. You're investing "after-tax" money. But...all future growth is never taxed. If you're over age 55, you can put almost $25,000 a year into a Roth 401(k).

BUT...not all employers offer a Roth 401(k). It's hard to understand why, but most do not. While I'm not a fan of most social protests these days, I'm fully supportive of one led by employees demanding inclusion of the Roth provision to their company's 401(k) plan. At least ask about it. It's not difficult or expensive.

But remember, switching from a traditional to a Roth 401(k) means more taxable income...and more income tax owed. This is why Step Four is so important. You must understand the cost of this strategy before you implement.

Fortunately, 401(k) contributions can be split between Roth and Traditional plans. It need not be all or nothing.

Step Five: Fund a Roth IRA if eligible.
If Sally doesn't have the Roth 401(k) option, she can invest $6,500 into a regular Roth, provided the Burns's combined contribution does not exceed the earnings limit. In 2018, it's $189,000 for married couples filing jointly.

Harry can do likewise, letting them contribute a combined $13,000.

Of course, this still leaves $77,000 of excess cash reserves. They could choose to invest that money for a higher return than a savings account. Or, they can continue moving toward a tax-free retirement with Step Six.

Step Six: Convert existing traditional IRAs to a Roth.
Harry has $250,000 of pre-tax money in a rollover IRA. Under current law, he can transfer as much

of it as he wants to a Roth IRA. Of course, whatever he transfers will be taxed, so I do NOT recommend he consider converting the full amount. The goal is to stay in their current bracket and to have enough cash on hand to pay the tax. Since conversions can be done incrementally, a multi-year strategy often works best.

I recommend you consider conversion to a Roth if you share one (or both) of the following concerns:

1.   A tax-free income during retirement or concerns of future rates rising.
2.   The desire to leave tax-free assets to heirs (that's right...your beneficiaries won't pay tax either on Roth accounts).

Step Seven: Use cash value life insurance.
Warning... Some consider controversial what I'm about to share. It's not.

A friend of mine likes to call life insurance "the most misunderstood asset class." Whether or not it is an asset class can be debated. But he is right in that there does exist a great deal of misunderstanding about it.

For 95% of all Americans, the purpose of life insurance is to replace income to dependents in the event of premature death. That's it. Mom or Dad passed away leaving a spouse and three rug rats in need of shelter, food, and clothing. And no matter what you read, Dave Ramsay is 100% correct when he recommends low-cost term insurance for income replacement. With it you get the most benefit for the least amount of cost.

The strategy that follows is for the other 5%.

A cash value life insurance policy is designed to be "insurance for life." You pay the necessary premiums and you'll never again have to take a health exam. Coverage is permanent. To be permanent, carriers much charge more money in the early years than they need to pay the eventual claim. A lot more. But don't worry. That extra premium is yours until the company needs it. And they'll credit you interest on that money, so it can grow.

Theoretically, the cash value in a policy could someday be worth a lot more than premiums paid provided there's enough interest credited to your account. Like I said...theoretically.

For example, let's say Harry purchased a policy back when he was in his mid 30's. He diligently placed $833 every month into the policy. By the time he reached age 55, he had paid in a total of $200,000. But the policy cash value is now worth $250,000 because of the credited interest. Not a great rate of return over the years, but remember the company had to withdraw some money every year to cover the cost of insurance.

The kids are all grown up, out of the house, and Harry wonders, "Do I even need this policy anymore." The death benefit is $500,000, so like most of us, Harry is worth more dead than alive.

There is no simple answer to this question, so let's consider his options:

1. *Cancel the policy.* He'll get a check for $250,0000 but will have to pay tax on the $50,000 of gain. Plus, he'll need to pay a 10% penalty ($5,0000) because he canceled the policy before reaching the age of 59.5 (Rule 72(t) strikes again). But, he could invest the money (which could create taxable income) or use the proceeds to pay for Roth conversions.

2. *Keep the policy and continue to pay the premiums (or not).* Over time, cash value will hopefully continue to grow. But if he cares only about the death benefit, Harry may be able to stop paying premiums all together and let the policy costs be serviced by the existing cash value. He'll need to contact his company to explore this option. Every policy is different.

3. *Draw income from the policy:* Most policies allow the owner to access the cash value without incurring tax on the growth. In Harry's case, the first $200,000 he takes will be considered a policy withdrawal, a return of his original money. No big deal. Not taxable. Should he wish to access the $50,000 of growth, he can do so tax-free via a policy loan. Loans are tax-free. Keep in mind that loans and withdrawals do affect the policy's long-term performance. So, be careful. Too much withdrawn can lower the death benefit and put the policy at risk of lapsing. But done properly, it can

provide a tax-free income stream. Harry needs to study his policy very carefully before proceeding.

Another life insurance option is to buy a new policy and fund it to create a desired tax-free income stream as described above. The tax code allows you to deposit into a policy far more money than is required to service it (although there is a limit). Be mindful that your actual return is unknown, the internal policy costs are real and will have a negative impact on your growth.

In recent years, life insurance carriers have added a new provision: long-term care. Simply put, the policy death benefit can be used as a living benefit to cover some or all the cost of long-term care. Combining cash value growth with long-term care coverage can essentially "kill two birds with one stone." An excellent book on this concept is Look Before You LIRP by David McKnight. *See Appendix VI for more information.*

Harry & Sally are Free

As Americans, it's easy for us to take freedom for granted. We can live where we want, say what we want, start a business. A perfect country? Of course not. People aren't perfect. So no country can be perfect.

We even have a constitution designed to limit the freedoms not of the people, but of the government. Originally, the government had no right to tax your ability to earn.

In 1997, President Clinton signed a bill creating only the second true tax haven for American savings: The Roth IRA. The first? Cash Value Life Insurance.

Today, Harry and Sally save half of their money in these two tax-free accounts.

Here's how we did it.

While still working, The Burns's combined income of $210,000 put them into the 24% marginal bracket. With their itemized deductions of

$40,000, they could earn another $145,000 before jumping to the 32% rate.

During each of the ten years before retirement, Harry and Sally converted Harry's entire 401(k) with his former employer to a Roth IRA. Also, Sally started to move 401(k) contributions from the traditional to the Roth IRA. Lastly, the Burns surrendered their term policies and bought two cash value policies for the same premium (but lower death benefits). The new policies have a long-term care rider.

Here's how their assets now look from a tax standpoint as they approach retirement:

When Will It Be Taxed?

Now?	Later?	Never?
$60,000	$650,000	$600,000

What's different? First off, the pre-tax net worth is smaller. $90,000 in cash was used to pay the cost of conversion over time. Secondly, half the money now sits in a taxed never account. The after-tax net worth, however, is considerably higher. Before the strategy, after-tax net worth was estimated to be $1,025,000. Now it's $1,150,000 assuming a 30% tax rate on taxed later assets.

Furthermore, they've protected almost half of their net worth against future tax increases. Should Harry and Sally wish to draw $3,000 a month from savings, all or part can come from their tax-free account. Doing so will allow them to have the income they desire and NOT have to pay tax on their Social Security.

Desired income: $72,000

Social Security: $36,000

Traditional IRA: $16,000

Roth IRA: $18,000

MAGI: $16,000 (Traditional IRA) + ½ $36,000 = $34,000

The MAGI doesn't exceed $34,000, so none of their Social Security benefit is taxed. Remember, Roth withdrawals do not count toward the MAGI.

Since the $16,000 from the traditional IRA is less than the $26,500 standard deduction, then Harry and Sally owe no taxes at all. They have a tax-free retirement.

If taxes should rise in the future, they can choose to take more from the Roth and less from the IRA. By age 70.5, however, they will be required to start taking minimum amounts from the IRA based on their age and account balance. So by taking some traditional IRA distributions now, they can lower their RMD in the future. And, as you can see in this example, those withdrawals are tax-free. *For more details on how the RMD works, see Appendix V.*

Your Turn

You choose to pay your taxes. No, I'm not suggesting you're free not to pay them. But how you structure your finances to minimize taxation is your business. As former US Judge Learned Hand so eloquently put it:

"Anyone may arrange his affairs so that his taxes shall be as low as possible; he is not bound to choose that pattern which best pays the treasury. There is not even a patriotic duty to increase one's taxes or public duty to pay more than the law demands."

Tax planning is complicated. The code itself has over 70,000 pages, full of nuances, exceptions, and confusion. Some might suggest it's Congress's way of getting people to pay more than they should.

If you knew your investments would drop 30% next week, would you do something about it? Of course you would. Well, if your money is sitting in a 401(k), it may already be worth 30% less than the value on your statement given the IRS lien resting on it.

The decision is whether or not it makes sense to take advantage of the present tax rates, possibly the lowest in your lifetime, or continue to kick the can down the road and hope our government suddenly adopts a habit of low taxes AND low spending.

At the very least, you owe it to yourself to explore your planning options. Take advantage of this free opportunity to meet with **Jerry and Nick** for a FREE one hour consultation:

Jerry Royer, RFC® and Nicholas Royer, MRFC

2600 Maitland Center Parkway
Suite 355
Maitland, FL 32751

info@group10financial.com

1-800-245-0546

www.group10financial.com

Appendix I: The Roth 401(k)

Under a regular 401(k), 403(b), or 457(b) governmental plan, a participant chooses to defer a portion of his or her compensation into the plan. Such "elective deferrals" are made on a pre-tax basis, any account growth is tax- deferred, and withdrawals are taxed as ordinary income.[1]

In a qualified Roth contribution program, a participant can choose to have all or part of his or her elective deferrals made to a separate, designated Roth account. Such "designated Roth contributions" are made on an after-tax basis. Growth in the designated Roth account is tax-deferred and qualified distributions are excluded from gross income.

Other points:

- Separate accounting and recordkeeping are required for the deferrals under the regular,

---

[1] The discussion here concerns federal income tax law. State or local income tax law may differ.

pre-tax portions of a plan and for those made to the after-tax, designated Roth account.

- Individuals whose adjusted gross income exceeds certain limits may not contribute to a regular Roth IRA. There are no such income limits applicable to a designated Roth account.

- For 401(k) plans, contributions to a designated Roth account are elective deferrals for purposes of the Actual Deferral Percentage (ADP) test.

Contributions

A number of rules apply to contributions to a qualified Roth contribution program:

- Dollar limitation: For 2018, a maximum of $18,500 may be contributed. Those who are age 50 and older may make additional contributions of $6,000. A participant may choose to place all of his or her contributions in the regular, pre-tax portion of a plan, all in the designated Roth account, or split the deferrals between the two.

- Employer contributions: Employer contributions will be credited only to the regular, pre-tax portion of a plan; they may not be designated as Roth contributions.

- Excess contributions: Excess deferrals to a designated Roth account must be distributed to the participant no later than April 15 of the year following the year in which the excess deferral was made. Otherwise, the excess deferral will be taxed twice, once in the year of deferral and a second time the year a corrective distribution is made.

Distributions

A distribution from a designated Roth account will be excluded from income if it is made at least five years after a contribution to such an account was first made and at least one of the following applies:

- The participant reaches age 59½;
- The participant dies;
- The participant becomes disabled.

Such distributions are known as "qualified" distributions.

Other points:

- Nonqualified distributions: If a distribution does not meet the above requirements, it is termed a "nonqualified" distribution. Such distributions are subject to federal income tax, including a 10% premature distribution penalty if the participant is under age 59½ in the year the funds are distributed. Such distributions are taxed under the annuity rules of IRC Sec. 72; any part of a distribution that is attributable to earnings is includable in income; any portion attributable to the original investment (basis) is recovered tax-free. This contrasts sharply with the taxation of nonqualified distributions from a regular Roth IRA account. Nonqualified distributions from a regular Roth IRA are taxed following pre-defined ordering rules under which basis is recovered first, followed by earnings.

- First-time homebuyer expenses: In a regular Roth IRA, a qualified distribution may be made to pay for first-time homebuyer expenses. This provision does not apply to distributions from a designated Roth account.

- Rollovers to designated Roth accounts: Distributions from the regular, pre-tax portion of a qualified plan may be rolled-over into a designated Roth account. The individual (either the participant or a surviving spouse) must include the distribution in gross income (subject to basis recovery) in the same manner as if the distribution from the pre-tax plan had been rolled over into a Roth IRA.

- Rollovers from designated Roth accounts: A distribution from a designated Roth account may only be rolled over into a Roth IRA or another designated Roth account. Such a rollover is not a taxable event.

- Required minimum distributions: Generally, amounts in a designated Roth account are subject to the required minimum distribution rules applicable to plan participants when they reach age 70½.

However, a participant can avoid the mandated distributions by rolling over amounts in the designated Roth account into a regular Roth IRA.

Which Account To Choose?

The decision as to which type of account should be used will generally be made on factors such as the length of time until retirement (or until the funds are needed), the amount of money available to contribute each year, the participant's current tax situation, and the anticipated marginal tax rate in retirement. An important issue to keep in mind is the overall, lifetime tax burden.

- Regular 401(k), 403(b), or 457(b) governmental plan: Generally, individuals with a relatively short period of time until retirement, or who expect that their marginal tax rate will be lower in retirement, will benefit more from a regular, pre-tax qualified retirement plan.

- Designated Roth account: Younger individuals with more years until retirement and those who anticipate that their marginal tax rate will rise in retirement will generally benefit more from a designated Roth account. The fact that contributions to a designated Roth account are after-tax may cause current cash-flow problems for some individuals. Higher income participants may find that taxable income will be higher with a designated Roth account than with a regular pre-tax plan, potentially reducing tax breaks such as the child tax credit or AMT exemption.

- Both: Some individuals may choose to contribute to both types of plan, to provide flexibility in retirement.

Seek Professional Guidance
Because of the complexities involved, the guidance of tax and financial professionals is strongly recommended.

Appendix II: Roth IRAs

The Roth IRA differs from the traditional IRA in that contributions are never deductible and, if certain requirements are met, account distributions are free of federal income tax.[1]

Funding a Roth IRA

Annual contributions: A Roth IRA may be established and funded at any time between January 1 of the current year, up to and including the date an individual's federal income tax return is due, (generally April 15 of the following year), not including extensions.

Conversion of a traditional IRA account:

A traditional IRA may be converted to a Roth IRA, with the conversion being a taxable event. For the year of conversion, the taxpayer must include in gross income previously deducted contributions plus net earnings (or minus net losses). For individual retirement annuities, gross income is generally increased by the fair market value of the contract on the date of conversion (through a re-designation) or distribution (if held inside an IRA). If a retirement annuity is completely surrendered, the cash received is the amount includable in income. Any 10% penalty tax for early withdrawal is waived. However, if a taxpayer withdraws amounts from the Roth IRA within five years of the conversion, the 10% penalty tax will apply to those amounts deemed to be part of the conversion, unless an exception applies.

Prior to 2018, a taxpayer who converted a traditional IRA to a Roth IRA could "undo" the transaction and "recharacterize" the converted funds, moving them back into a traditional IRA.

However, for tax years beginning in 2018, the Tax Cuts and Jobs Act of 2017 (TCJA), permanently repealed the ability to recharacterize a Roth conversion back to a traditional IRA.

TCJA did not repeal the ability of a taxpayer to convert a Roth IRA to a traditional IRA and then recharacterize the converted funds, moving them back into a Roth IRA.

Rollovers from a qualified plan:
Distributions from qualified retirement plans, IRC Sec. 457(b) governmental plans, and IRC Sec. 403(b) plans may also be rolled over to a Roth IRA.

These conversions are taxable events, with gross income for the year of conversion being increased by previously deducted contributions plus net earnings (or minus net losses).

Direct rollover from a designated Roth Account:
Funds may be rolled into a regular Roth IRA from a designated Roth account that is part of a 401(k), 403(b), or 457(b) governmental plan. Such a rollover is not a taxable event and the filing status and MAGI limitations normally applicable to regular Roth contributions do not apply.

Military death payments:
Under the provisions of the Heroes Earnings Assistance and Relief Tax Act of 2008, an individual who receives a military death gratuity and/or a payment under the Servicemembers' Group Life Insurance (SGLI) program may contribute to a Roth IRA an amount no greater than the sum of any military death gratuity and SGLI payment. Such a contribution is considered a qualified rollover contribution and must be made within one year of receiving the death gratuity or insurance payment. The annual dollar contribution limit and income-based phase-out of the dollar contribution limit do not apply to such contributions.

Type of Arrangements Permitted

There are currently two types of Roth IRAs.

- Individual retirement accounts: Trusts or custodial accounts with a corporate trustee or custodian.

- Individual retirement annuities: Special annuities issued by a life insurance company.

Contribution Limits

Limits: For 2018, an individual may contribute (but not deduct) the lesser of $5,500 or 100% of compensation[2] for the year. For a married couple, an additional $5,500 may be contributed on behalf of a lesser earning (or nonworking) spouse, using a spousal account.

A husband and wife may contribute up to a total of $11,000, as long as their combined compensation is at least that amount.[3]

---

[2] "Compensation" includes taxable wages, salaries, or commissions or the net income from self-employment
[3] These amounts apply to 2018. For 2017, the maximum allowable contribution was also $5,500 for a single individual and $11,000 for a married couple.

If an IRA owner is age 50 or older, he or she may contribute an additional $1,000 ($2,000 if the spouse is also age 50 or older).

Other IRAs: The contribution limits for a Roth IRA are coordinated with those of a traditional IRA; a taxpayer may not contribute more than the annual limit for that tax year into a single IRA or a combination of traditional and Roth IRAs. Excess contributions to a traditional or Roth IRA are subject to a 6% excise tax.

Contribution phase out: For 2018, the maximum contribution to a Roth IRA is phased out for single taxpayers with MAGI between $120,000 and $135,000. For married couples filing jointly, the phase-out range is a MAGI of $189,000 to $199,000. For married individuals filing separately, the phase-out range is a MAGI of $0 to $10,000.[4]

Taxation of Distributions

A distribution from a Roth IRA that is a "qualified" distribution is excluded from gross income and is

---

[4] For 2017, the phase-out ranges were: (1) MFJ – MAGI of $186,000 - $196,000 and (2) Single - $118,000 - $133,000. For those using the MFS filing status, the phase-out range is $0 - $10,000, which does not change.

not subject to federal income tax. A distribution is qualified if it is made after a five- year waiting period[5] and at least one of the following requirements is met:

- after the taxpayer reaches age 59½; or
- due to the taxpayer's death; or
- because the taxpayer becomes disabled; or
- to pay for first-time-home-buyer expenses up to $10,000.

The earnings portion of a "non-qualified" distribution is subject to tax. To determine any taxable distribution, the funds are considered to be withdrawn in a specified order:

- Any withdrawal is considered to come first from nondeductible contributions, which are not subject to tax.

- After all contributions have been withdrawn, any conversion amounts are considered next. A distribution of converted funds is not included in gross income, but may be subject to the 10% premature distribution penalty if the funds are

---

[5] Generally, five years after a contribution is first made, or amounts are converted to a Roth IRA.

withdrawn within five years of being converted.

- Once all contributions and conversions have been withdrawn, any remaining funds are deemed to be earnings, and, when distributed, are included in gross income.

Premature Distributions

If a taxable distribution is received prior to age 59½, a 10% penalty tax is added to the regular income tax due, unless one or more of the following exceptions apply:

- A distribution is made because of the death or disability of the account owner.

- A withdrawal is part of a scheduled series of substantially equal periodic payments.

- A distribution is rolled-over into another Roth IRA.

- A withdrawal is used to pay for deductible medical expenses.

- The distribution is used to pay for certain qualified higher-education expenses.

- Amounts are withdrawn to pay for first-time homebuyer expenses of up to $10,000.

- In certain situations, to pay health insurance premiums for unemployed individuals.

- Distributions by certain military reservists called to active duty after 09/11/2001.

- A distribution is transferred to a Health Savings Account (HSA).

- In case of an IRS levy on the account.

Other Differences

There are several other significant differences between the traditional and Roth IRAs:

Contributions after age 70½: Contributions to a Roth IRA may be made even after the taxpayer has reached age 70½, as long as the taxpayer has compensation at least equal to the contribution, subject to the phase-out rules.

Distribution requirements: Roth IRAs are not subject to the mandatory required minimum distribution (RMD) rules during the life of the owner (triggered at age 70½) applicable to traditional IRAs. However, there are post-death minimum distribution rules applicable to non-spousal beneficiaries who inherit a Roth account.

Charitable Distributions

Federal income tax law provides for an exclusion from gross income of up to $100,000 for distributions made from a Roth or traditional IRA directly to a qualified charitable organization. Such a distribution counts towards the taxpayer's RMD requirements. The IRA owner (Or beneficiary of an inherited IRA) must be at least age 70½ when the distribution is made. No charitable deduction is allowed for such a qualified charitable distribution.

Transfers to Health Savings Accounts (HSAs)

Federal law allows for a limited, one-time, direct transfer of funds from an IRA to an HSA. If certain requirements are met, any otherwise taxable portion of the distribution is excluded from income and the 10% early distribution penalty will not apply.

Investment Alternatives

- Banks, savings and loans, credit unions: Certificates of deposit in Roth IRAs are generally insured by either the FDIC or the NCUA for amounts up to $250,000. Fixed and variable rates are available. There may be stiff penalties for early withdrawal.

- Annuities: Traditional, fixed individual retirement annuities issued by life insurance companies can guarantee fixed monthly income at retirement and may include a disability-waiver-of-premium provision. Variable annuities do not guarantee a fixed monthly income at retirement.

- Money market: Yield fluctuates with the economy. Investor cannot lock in higher interest rates. It is easy to switch to other investments.

- Mutual funds: A wide variety of mutual funds with many investment objectives are available.

- Zero coupon bonds: Bonds are issued at a deep discount from face value. There are no worries about reinvesting interest payments. Zero coupon bonds are subject to inflation risk and interest rate risk.

- Stocks: A wide variety of investments (and risk) is possible. Losses are generally not deductible.
- Limited partnerships:
  Some limited partnerships are especially designed for qualified plans, specifically in the areas of real estate and mortgage pools.

Prohibited Investments or Transactions

- Life insurance: Roth IRAs cannot include life insurance contracts.

- Loans to IRA taxpayer: Self-borrowing triggers a constructive distribution of the entire amount in an IRA.

- Collectibles: Purchase of art works, antiques, metals, gems, stamps, etc., will be treated as a taxable distribution. Coins issued under state law and certain U.S. gold, silver and platinum coins are exceptions. Certain kinds of bullion may be purchased.

Other Factors to Consider

- What is the yield? More frequent compounding will produce a higher return. Is the interest rate fixed or variable? If interest rates drop, a fixed rate may be better, especially if you can make future contributions at the same fixed rate. If interest rates go up, you may be able to roll the account to another Roth IRA.

- How often can you change investments? Is there a charge?

- Refunds of federal income taxes may be directly deposited into an IRA.

- Federal bankruptcy law protects assets in Roth IRA accounts, up to $1,283,025.[6] Funds rolled over from qualified plans are protected without limit.

---

[6] Effective April 1, 2016. The limit is indexed for inflation every three years.

Appendix III: Roth IRA Conversion Factors to Consider

Before 2010, taxpayers[7] with a modified adjusted gross income (MAGI)[8] in excess of $100,000, or who filed their federal income tax returns using the Married Filing Separately filing status, were prohibited from converting a traditional IRA to a Roth IRA. Beginning in 2010, however, these prohibitions no longer applied. For many individuals, the ability to convert a traditional IRA to a Roth IRA represents a significant tax planning opportunity.[9]

---

[7] The discussion here concerns federal income tax law. State or local law may differ.

[8] Modified adjusted gross income (MAGI) is a taxpayer's adjusted gross income (AGI) with certain deductions or exclusions added back. For most taxpayers, MAGI and AGI are the same.

[9] Although the discussion here focuses on traditional IRAs, the same rules apply to amounts converted from a SEP IRA or SIMPLE IRA to a Roth IRA. Funds in a SIMPLE IRA that do not meet the two-year period described in IRC Sec. 72(t)(6) may not be converted. Distributions from IRC Sec. 401(a) qualified retirement plans, IRC Sec. 457(b) governmental plans, and IRC Sec. 403(b) plans may also be rolled over into a Roth IRA.

Pay Me Later or Pay Me Now

With a traditional IRA, and assuming certain requirements are met, contributions are deductible in the year they are made. The tax due on the contributions, and the tax due on any earnings or growth, is deferred until funds are distributed from the account, typically at retirement. From an income tax perspective, this is a "pay me later" scenario.

With a Roth IRA, contributions are never deductible; they are made with funds that have already been taxed. If certain requirements are met, both the contributions and any earnings or growth are received income-tax free when withdrawn from the account. From an income tax perspective, this is a "pay me now" scenario.

A taxpayer who elects to convert a traditional IRA to a Roth IRA has chosen to pay the income tax now rather than waiting until the future to pay it. To justify a conversion, the benefit of not paying taxes tomorrow should be greater than the cost of paying taxes today.

Benefits of Roth IRAs

The benefits of holding assets in a Roth IRA can be considerable:

- During life - tax-free income:
  Assuming that certain requirements are met, including a five-taxable year waiting period after a contribution is first made to a Roth IRA for the owner, "qualified" distributions are received income-tax free.

- At death – income-tax free to beneficiaries:
  At death, the value of the Roth IRA is includable in the account owner's estate, subject to federal estate tax. A surviving spouse can treat an inherited Roth IRA as his or her own, with the proceeds being received income-tax free, and with no required minimum distributions. For non-spousal beneficiaries, and assuming that the five-year waiting period requirement has been met, the proceeds are received income-tax free. After the owner's death, however, non-spousal beneficiaries must take certain required minimum distributions.

- No lifetime required minimum distributions: Federal income tax law mandates that certain required minimum distributions be made from traditional IRAs, beginning when the account owner reaches age 70½. For Roth IRAs, there are no minimum distribution requirements during the lifetime of the account owner.

- Contributions after age 70½: As long as a taxpayer has "compensation" (such as wages or self-employment income), contributions may be made to a Roth IRA regardless of the taxpayer's age, subject to the modified adjusted gross income limitations. No contributions are permitted to a traditional IRA for any year in which the owner is age 70½ or older.

The Cost of Conversion

Converting a traditional IRA to a Roth IRA is a currently taxable event. For the year the converted assets are distributed, the taxpayer must include in gross income all previously deducted contributions, plus net earnings (or minus net losses). For individual retirement annuities, gross income is generally increased by the fair market value of the contract on the date of conversion (through a re-designation) or distribution (if held inside an IRA). If a retirement annuity is completely surrendered, the cash received is the amount includable in income. Any 10% penalty tax for early withdrawal is waived.

If a taxpayer has traditional IRA accounts that hold both deductible and non-deductible amounts, he or she may not "cherry-pick" and convert only the non-deductible contributions.[10] Instead, the value of all IRA accounts is added together and a ratio is calculated to determine the tax-free portion of any conversion.[11]

Example: Paul has a traditional IRA to which he has made $20,000 in non-deductible contributions. This year, when he converts the account to a Roth IRA, the balance in this IRA is $30,000. Paul also has a separate IRA containing $70,000 in pre-tax contributions rolled over from a 401(k) plan with a previous employer. The total

---

[10] Because they have already been taxed, non-deductible contributions are generally not taxable when converted from a traditional IRA to a Roth IRA.

[11] If all of the contributions to the traditional IRA were deductible, a taxpayer may elect to roll over everything, or pick and choose which accounts or portions of an account to convert.

value of both accounts is $100,000. His "non-deductible" ratio is thus 20%, ($20,000 ÷ $100,000). When Paul converts the $30,000 in his non-deductible IRA, he may exclude only $6,000 (20% x $30,000) from gross income. The remaining $24,000 ($30,000 - $6,000) is includable in his gross income, subject to tax.

Situations Favoring Conversion to A Roth IRA
- Small account values: If the dollar amount in the traditional IRA is small, the income-tax cost to convert today would be relatively low.
- Longer time to retirement: A longer period of time until retirement allows for greater future growth, necessary to recoup the up-front cost of paying the tax now.
- Cash to pay the taxes: Where will the money come from to pay the extra taxes? It's usually better if the account owner has sufficient cash outside of the IRA to pay the tax. Could the funds used to pay the tax today provide a greater return if invested elsewhere?
- IRA income not needed: Some individuals have adequate retirement income from

other sources, so that IRA monies are not needed to fund retirement. During the lifetime of the account owner, a Roth IRA has no minimum distribution requirements.

- Higher future tax bracket: If a taxpayer anticipates being in a higher tax bracket in the future, paying the tax today, at lower rates, is a logical step. Being taxed at a higher marginal rate may be the result of legislative changes, having a higher taxable income, or a change in filing status, such as when a couple divorces or a spouse dies.

Situations NOT Favoring Conversion
In some situations, converting a traditional IRA to a Roth IRA may not be appropriate:

- Retirement begins soon: If there is only a short time before retirement begins, there may not be enough time for future growth to offset the cost of paying the tax today.

- High IRA account values: If the dollar amount in the traditional IRA is large, the tax bill resulting from the conversion will likely be expensive; the conversion could push a taxpayer into a higher marginal tax bracket or make Social Security benefits taxable.

- No cash to pay the taxes: A taxpayer may not have the cash outside the IRA to pay the extra tax that results from the conversion. Taking funds from the IRA to pay the increased tax reduces the amount left in the account to grow into the future. If the account owner is under age 59½ at the time these extra funds are withdrawn from the IRA, a 10% penalty on the amount not converted will likely be added to the tax bill.

- Lower future tax rates: If a taxpayer anticipates being in a lower tax bracket in the future, paying the tax today, at higher marginal tax rates, makes no sense.

Recharacterization
Prior to 2018, a taxpayer who converted a traditional IRA to a Roth IRA could "undo" the transaction and "recharacterize" the converted funds, moving them back into a traditional IRA.

However, for tax years beginning in 2018, the Tax Cuts and Jobs Act of 2017 (TCJA), permanently repealed the ability to recharacterize a Roth conversion back to a traditional IRA.

Seek Professional Guidance
The decision to convert all or part of a traditional IRA to a Roth IRA is an individual one. A thorough analysis requires careful consideration of a number of income tax, investment, and estate planning factors, over an extended time horizon. The advice and guidance of appropriate financial, tax, and investment professionals is strongly recommended.

Appendix IV: IRC Sec. 72(t)(2)(A)(iv)

Generally, taxable distributions from employer-sponsored qualified retirement plans, and from traditional and Roth IRAs, made before the account owner reaches age 59½, are subject to a 10% "early" withdrawal penalty.[12] One exception to this 10% penalty is for distributions taken as a series of "substantially equal periodic payments."

This exception applies to distributions made, at least once a year, over the life (or life expectancy) of the participant, or over the joint lives (or joint life expectancies) of the participant and a beneficiary. The payments must continue unchanged (except for death or disability) for the longer of: (a) five years (five years from the date of the first payment), or (b) the participant reaches age 59½. Otherwise, the 10% penalty will be applied retroactively and interest will be charged.

---

[12] The discussion here concerns federal income tax law. State or local law may differ. Under federal law, the 10% penalty generally applies to distributions which are includable in gross income

Calculating the Substantially-Equal Periodic Payment

In Notice 89-25, 11989-1, CB 662, Q&A-12 (March 20, 1989), the IRS listed three acceptable methods of calculating such a distribution:

- Required minimum distribution (RMD): The annual payment is determined using a method acceptable for calculating the required minimum distribution required under IRC Sec. 401(a)(9). In general, the account balance is divided by a life expectancy factor, resulting in a payment which changes from year to year.
- Fixed amortization method: Payment under this method is similar to the annual amount required to pay off a loan (equal to the amount in the plan at the start of distributions), at a reasonable interest rate, over the remainder of one's life. The dollar amount of the payment remains the same in each subsequent year.
- Fixed annuitization: An annuity factor is determined from a reasonable mortality table at an interest rate which is then reasonable for the age of the recipient of the distribution. The payment is determined

for the first distribution and remains the same in each subsequent year.

Revenue Ruling 2002-62

On October 3, 2002, the IRS released Revenue Ruling 2002-62, to address questions raised by taxpayers who had begun to receive distributions under IRC Sec. 72(t)(2)(A)(iv) and who had been adversely affected by a declining stock market. This ruling contained the following key points.

- It expanded the guidance given in Q&A 12 of IRS Notice 89-25 to, among other things, incorporate into the calculation process the new life expectancy tables issued in April, 2002, with regard to required minimum distributions from IRAs and qualified plans.
- Allowed a participant who had been using either the fixed amortization method or the fixed annuitization method to make a one-time change to the RMD method.
- Specified that if a participant who is using an acceptable method to calculate the required substantially equal periodic payments exhausts the assets in an account prior to the required time period, the

"cessation of payments will not be treated as a modification of the series of payments."

The guidance provided in Revenue Ruling 2002-62 replaced the guidance of IRS Notice 89-25 for any series of payments beginning on or after January 1, 2003. If distributions began before 2003 under any method that satisfied IRC Sec. 72(t)(2)(A)(iv), a change to the required minimum distribution calculation method may be made at any time.

Comparing the Three Methods[13]
Assumptions:

Plan or IRA account balance on 12/31 of the previous year: $400,000
Age of participant in distribution year: 50
Single life expectancy at age 50: 34.2[14]
Interest rate assumed: 2.98%[15]
Distribution period: Single life only

Required minimum distribution method:
For the current year, the annual distribution amount is calculated by dividing account balance by the participant's life expectancy.

$$\$400,000 \ / \ 34.2 = \$11,696$$

---

[13] The examples shown are from the IRS web site, www.irs.gov, "Retirement Plans FAQs Regarding Substantially Equal Periodic Payments," August 4, 2017.

[14] Derived from the Single Life Table found in Reg.1.401(a)(9)-9, Q&A-1. The Uniform Lifetime Table found in Appendix A of Revenue Ruling 2002-62 or the Joint and Last Survivor table of Reg.1.401(a)(9)-9, Q&A-3 may also be used.

[15] This rate is equal to 120% of the federal mid-term rate. In these IRS examples, the rate for April 2011 is used. This value will fluctuate and changes monthly.

Fixed amortization method:
Distribution amount is calculated by amortizing the account balance over the number of years of the participant's single life expectancy. The calculation is the same as in determining the payment required to pay off a loan.

$$\$400,000 \times (.0298 / (1 - (1 + .0298)^{-34.2}))$$
$$= \$18,811$$

Fixed annuitization method:
The distribution amount is equal to the account balance divided by an annuity factor that for the present value of an annuity of one dollar per year paid over the life of a 50-year-old participant. Such annuity factors are typically calculated by an actuary. In this case, the age-50 annuity factor (21.345) is based on the mortality table in Appendix B of Revenue Ruling 2002-62 and an interest rate of 2.98%.

$$\$400,000 / 21.345 = \$18,740$$

Method	Annual Withdrawal
Required minimum distribution	$11,696
Fixed amortization	$18,811
Fixed annuitization	$18,740

Appendix V: Cash Value Life Insurance

Accumulating Funds to Meet Savings Goals
Saving money to reach an accumulation goal is a problem many of us face. Some goals, such as retirement or a college fund for a child, are long-term savings goals. Many of us also have shorter-term savings goals such as a vacation or a Christmas or holiday fund.

Whatever the objective, the basic problem is the same, i.e. where to put money aside to reach a particular savings goal. For many short-term goals, a savings account at a local bank or credit union is a popular choice. For college funding, Coverdell IRAs or IRC Sec. 529 plans are often used. For retirement savings, many individuals depend on Individual Retirement Accounts (IRAs) or employer-sponsored retirement plans such as an IRC Sec. 401(k) plan.

An additional option for long-term savings, one that is sometimes overlooked, is using a cash value life insurance policy.

What is Cash Value Life Insurance?

Life insurance comes in two basic variations, "term" insurance and "cash value" life insurance. Term life insurance can be compared to auto insurance. Protection is provided for a specified period of time or "term." No death benefits are paid unless the insured dies during the term the policy is in force. If the insured lives beyond the term period, the policy generally expires with nothing returned to the policy owner.

In addition to providing a death benefit, "cash value" life insurance also provides for the tax-deferred accumulation of money inside the policy. These funds can be used by the policy owner while the insured is alive to provide the resources for needs such as funding a college education, making improvements to the home, or starting a business. When the policy owner uses the cash values to meet such needs, he or she is said to have used the "living benefits" of a cash value life insurance policy.

When to Consider Cash Value Life Insurance

Using a cash value life insurance policy to reach a saving goal works best in certain situations:

- A need for life insurance death benefit apart from the need for additional savings, an individual should have a need for the death benefit that life insurance provides. For example, such a need exists when an individual has a dependent spouse or children who would suffer economically if the individual died. Someone with a large estate might need additional cash at death to pay estate and other taxes as well as final expenses.

- Other savings aren't enough: Because of limitations in federal tax law,[16] other accumulation vehicles might not allow enough money to be put aside to meet a particular savings goal.

- Time frame: Ideally, there should be at least 10 to 15 years between today and the time the money will be needed. Because of mortality expenses and other policy charges, significant cash value accumulations are generally deferred until a policy has been in force for a number of

[16] The discussion here concerns federal income tax law. State or local tax law may vary widely.

years. Additionally, federal income tax law affects the design of cash value life insurance policies as well as the taxation of cash value withdrawals in the early years a policy is in force.

- Insurable: The insured needs to be healthy enough to have a policy issued on his or her life.

- An ongoing obligation: Cash value life insurance policies tend to have a higher premium cost than comparable term life policies. Paying the premiums over a number of years represents an ongoing financial obligation, to both keep the policy in force and achieve the savings goal.

Income Tax Considerations

There are a number of income tax issues to keep in mind when considering any life insurance policy. The death benefit payable under a life insurance contract because of the death of the insured is generally received income-tax free. Federal income taxation of life insurance "living benefits" is more complicated:

- Tax-deferred growth: The growth of cash value inside a life insurance policy is tax-deferred.

- Cost recovery rule: Amounts withdrawn from a cash-value life insurance contract are included in gross income (and become subject to tax) only when they exceed the policy owner's basis in the policy. This basis is also known as the "investment in the contract." This effectively treats withdrawals from the policy first as a non-taxable return of premium and secondly as taxable income.

- Investment in the contract: The total of all premiums paid less any policy dividends and any other prior tax-free distributions received.

- Policy dividends: Some "participating" life policies pay what are termed "dividends." Such dividends are a return of a portion of the policy owner's previously paid premiums. Policy dividends are not taxable until they exceed the owner's basis in the life insurance contract.

- Policy loans: Some cash value life insurance policies allow the policy owner to borrow at interest a portion of the accumulated cash value. While a policy is in force, policy loans are generally not taxable. However, if a policy is surrendered with a loan outstanding, taxable income will result to the extent that the unpaid loan amount exceeds the owner's basis in the contract.

- Modified Endowment Contracts (MECs): Some life insurance policies – primarily because there are large premium payments in the early years of the contract – are termed "Modified Endowment Contracts," or MECs. Under federal income tax law, distributions from a policy considered to be a MEC are treated differently than distributions from non- MEC policies. Withdrawals from a MEC (including a policy loan) will first be taxed as current income until all of the policy earnings have been taxed. If the owner is under age 59½, a 10% penalty also applies, unless the payments are due to disability or are annuity type payments. Once all policy earnings have been distributed (and taxed), any further withdrawals are treated as a non-taxable return of premium.

Accessing the Contract's Cash Values
When the time comes to use the accumulated cash values, withdrawals from the policy should be done in such a way as to avoid current income taxation (to the extent possible) and keep the policy in force.

- Withdrawal to basis: Initially a policy owner can take withdrawals (partial policy surrenders) until he or she has withdrawn an amount equal to the basis in the policy.

- Switching to policy loans: Once the basis has been withdrawn, the policy owner then begins using non-taxable policy loans. The interest payable on these policy loans is typically much less than a loan from a commercial bank or credit union.

- A combination: A policy owner can also use a combination of withdrawals and policy loans.

- Caveats: There are a number of issues that a policy owner needs to keep in mind:

- Withdrawals reduce the death benefit available under the policy.

- If an insured dies with a policy loan outstanding, the policy's death benefit is reduced by the amount of the loan balance.

- Excessive use of withdrawals and policy loans can result in the policy lapsing. Such a lapse can result in unexpected, negative tax results as well as the loss of a valuable financial asset.

A Multi-function Tool

Used appropriately, cash value life insurance can serve as financial tool with multiple uses. It can be used, in conjunction with more traditional savings vehicles, as a way to accumulate funds for long-term savings goals. At the same time the policy can, if the insured dies, provide a death benefit when the funds are most needed.

Seek Professional Guidance

Determining the appropriate amount of life insurance, the best type of policy to meet the needs of an individual's specific situation, and planning when and how to access a policy's cash values can be complex and confusing. The advice and guidance of trained insurance, tax, and other financial professionals is strongly recommended.

Appendix VI: Life Insurance – LTC Combination Policies

Providing for health care is a key part of retirement planning. For most Americans age 65 and over, the federal government's Medicare program, and its various components, provides most of the resources to take care of a typical retiree's health care needs.

One health care need that is only minimally covered by Medicare is that of long-term care (LTC). LTC is the term used to describe a variety of maintenance or "custodial" services required by individuals who are chronically disabled, ill, or infirm. Depending on individual needs, LTC may include nursing home care, assisted living, home health care, or adult day care.

Not everyone will need LTC in retirement. For those that do, LTC is expensive. In 2017, for example, the national median cost for a resident in an assisted living facility was $45,000 per year; the national median cost for a semi-private nursing home room was $85,755 per year.[17] The problem, then, is how to pay for an expensive need that may, or may not, occur.

One answer has been that of a stand-alone, long-term care insurance policy. Should the need arise, a LTC policy can furnish some or all of the resources needed to pay for care. LTC insurance can be expensive, however, and most policies allow for the possibility of future rate increases. Plus, if an individual uses few (or none) of a policy's benefits, there is a sense that the money was not well spent.

One alternative to a traditional LTC insurance policy is that of a "combination" policy that links a cash-value life insurance policy with a tax-qualified, long-term care benefit. These combination policies take advantage of federal[18] income tax law which allows for payment of "accelerated death benefits," up to the policy's death benefit, should the insured need long- term care. If LTC services are required, the policy death benefit can be used to help pay these costs. If LTC

---

[17] Source: The Genworth 2017 Cost of Care Summary, page 2.
[18] The discussion here concerns federal income tax law. State of local income tax law may differ.

services are not needed, or only a portion of the death benefit is used to pay LTC expenses, any remaining policy death benefit (less any policy loans) passes to beneficiaries named by the insured. Such a combination policy is most appropriate when there is a need for both life insurance and long-term care protection.

- Long-term care "riders": In return for paying an additional premium, a "rider" can be added to a life insurance policy which allows the insurance carrier to advance the policy's death benefit to the insured, if long-term care is required. With some policies, a second rider can be added to increase the total dollar amount available to pay for LTC services, beyond the policy's original death benefit.

- Benefit "triggers": Under federal law, tax-free, accelerated death benefits can be paid from the policy when the insured is considered to be either "terminally ill" (death is expected within 24 months) or "chronically ill." For long-term care purposes,[19]1 an insured is considered to be

---

[19] See IRC. Sec. 7702(b).

chronically ill when he or she is either (1) expected to be unable to perform for 90 days two of six activities of daily living (eating, toileting, transferring, bathing, dressing, and maintaining continence), or (2) suffers from a cognitive impairment such as Alzheimer's, dementia, or Parkinson's disease. With some policies, a more restrictive definition requires the underlying chronic condition to be permanent.

- Elimination period: Once the insured is determined to qualify, long-term care payments can begin after a waiting, or "elimination" period, which can range from 60- 100 days. The elimination period usually only has to be satisfied one time.

- Monthly LTC benefit amount: The monthly LTC benefit is a set percentage of the total death benefit, typically selected by the policy owner when the policy is purchased.

The table below shows the payment amount and length of time for a hypothetical policy with a $100,000 death benefit:

Payout Percentage	Exemption Amount	Payout Length
1%	$1,000 per month	100 months
2%	$2,000 per month	50 months
3%	$3,000 per month	33 months
4%	$4,000 per month	25 months
5%	$5,000 per month	20 months

- Effect of LTC payments on policy death benefit: As LTC benefits are paid out, the policy's death benefit is reduced dollar-for-dollar.

- Indemnity vs. actual expenses: Some policies pay benefits on an indemnity or cash basis, meaning that once payments begin the monthly payment is the same regardless of the dollar amount of LTC expenses incurred. Policies that pay benefits on an expense basis pay the lesser of the monthly benefit or the actual LTC expenses incurred. If LTC expenses are less than the normal monthly payment, any unused balance is held over, potentially extending the benefit period.

- Paying for the policy: In many cases, a life insurance policy with LTC benefits is funded with a large, single premium. A few policies are paid through periodic premium payments. If appropriate, an existing cash-value life insurance may be exchanged tax-free for a new combination policy.

- Underwriting: Some policies, typically those funded with a large, single premium, use a streamlined, simplified underwriting process, with no medical exam. Other policies may require a medical exam and a complete health history.

- Taxability of benefits: Depending on the type of policy, long-term care benefits are received income-tax free under either IRC Sec. 101(g) or IRC Sec. 7702B.

- Rate guarantees: With many life insurance policies, because the death benefit is a pre-defined amount, the premiums are often guaranteed not to change. With a few types of life insurance, the premium rates may increase under certain conditions, but normally within a specified range.

- Guaranteed return of premium: Certain single-premium policies provide for a return of the premium paid (within a specified period of time) if the insured decides not to keep the policy. Life insurance policies which are paid for through periodic payments typically do not have this feature.

- Residual death benefit: In some instance, a policy may include a "residual" death benefit. If this feature is included, even though the policy's death benefits are exhausted through LTC benefit payments, the policy will still pay a small amount (typically 5% - 10% of the initial death benefit) at the insured's death. This benefit allows the survivors to pay for funeral and other final expenses.

Other Factors to Consider

There are a number of other factors to keep in mind when considering a life insurance-LTC combination policy:

- Not considered state "partnership" LTC policies: Life-insurance-LTC combination policies generally do not qualify as state "partnership" LTC policies. An insured individual with a partnership LTC policy can keep a much larger dollar amount of assets, while still qualifying for Medicaid, once the partnership LTC policy benefits are exhausted. Normally, an individual must be nearly destitute before Medicaid will pay for long-term care.

- Effect of inflation: Over time, the cost of LTC, like many other things that we buy, will increase. Since it may be many years in the future before long-term care is needed, consider a combination policy that offers a cost-of-living (COLI) rider. Without such a rider, there is a risk that a policy's LTC benefits will not keep up with increases in the cost of long-term care. Generally, once a policy is in force, the death benefit does not increase. Certain types of policies (variable life, variable universal life) have a death benefit that may increase, depending on investment results.

- Most funded with a large, single premium: Most life insurance-LTC combination policies are funded with a large, single premium payment. In many instances, a minimum of $25,000 - $75,000 is required to purchase a significant LTC benefit amount.

- Is this the right tool? A combination life insurance-LTC combination may not be the right tool if, for example, the insured is already covered by adequate life insurance. If there is a potential need for additional retirement income, a deferred annuity-LTC combination may be a better fit. For some individuals, a stand-alone LTC policy is more appropriate.

Seek Professional Guidance
One key part of a well-prepared retirement plan is looking ahead to the possible need for long-term care. The advice and guidance of trained financial and insurance professionals, in sorting out the various options for meeting this need, is strongly recommended.

Made in the USA
Lexington, KY
14 November 2019